D0603356

Lo, Rich,
Chinese New Year colors
/
[2019]
mi
01/03/20

春节
的
颜
色

CHINESE NEW YEAR COLORS

RICH LO

HOLIDAY HOUSE · NEW YORK

Copyright © 2019 by Richard Lo
All Rights Reserved

HOLIDAY HOUSE is registered in the U.S. Patent and Trademark Office.
Printed and bound in May 2019 at Tien Wah Press, Johor Bahru, Johor, Malaysia.
www.holidayhouse.com
First Edition
1 3 5 7 9 10 8 6 4 2

Library of Congress Cataloging-in-Publication Data

Names: Lo, Rich, author, illustrator.
Title: Chinese New Year colors / Rich Lo.
Description: First Edition. | New York : HOLIDAY HOUSE. [2019] | Audience:
   Ages: 3–7. | Audience: Grades: K to Grade 3. | Colors identified in both
   English and Chinese.
Identifiers: LCCN 2019014091 | ISBN 9780823443710 (Hardcover)
Subjects: LCSH: Chinese New Year—Juvenile literature. | Colors—Juvenile
   literature. | New Year—China—Juvenile literature. | China—Social life
   and customs—Juvenile literature.
Classification: LCC GT4905 .L566 2019 | DDC 394.261—dc23
   LC record available at https://lccn.loc.gov/2019014091

Dedicated to my parents,
who kept the family together through
tough times in a country and culture
they knew very little about.

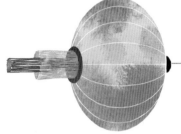

Red

Hồng ẾT Hồng

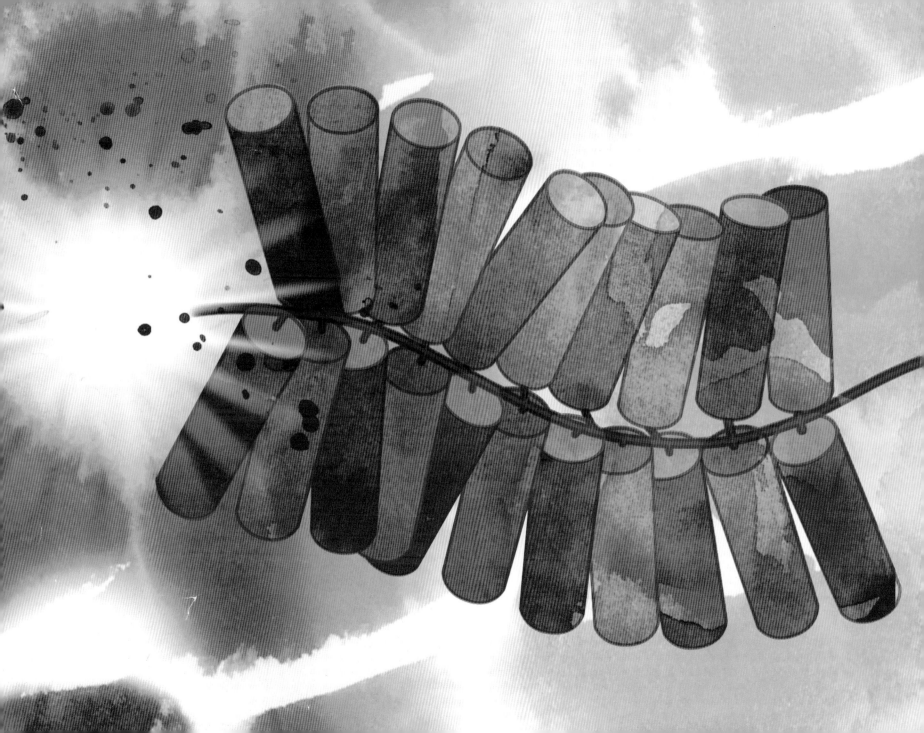

Blue

藍 Lán

Orange

橙 Chéng

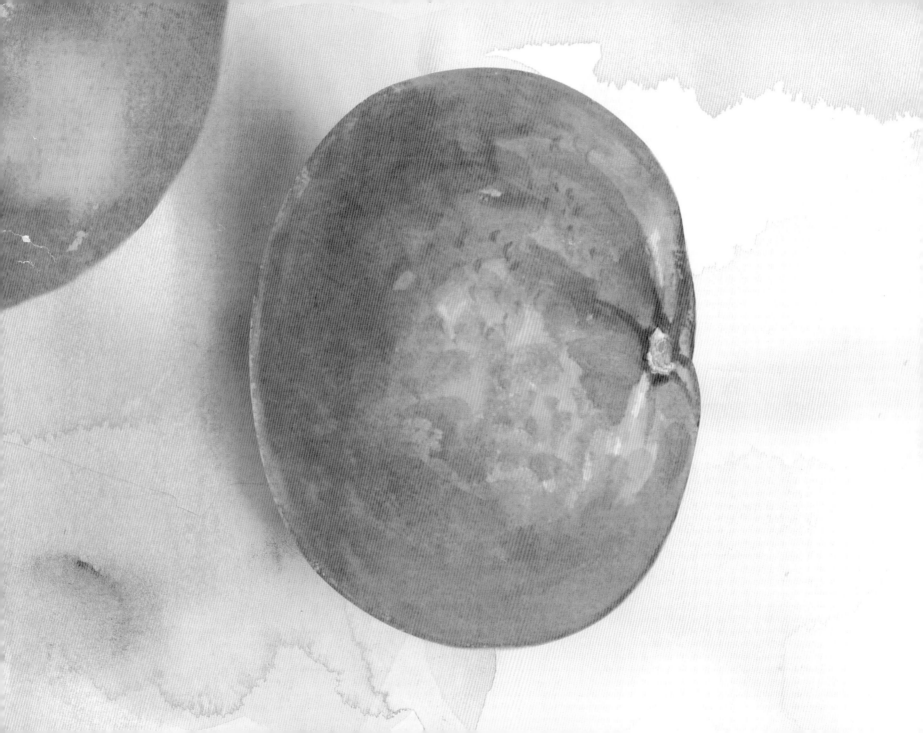

Yellow

Huáng

黄

Green

绿 Lü

Pink

Fěn Hóng

粉
红

Cerulean

Qiǎn lán

浅蓝

Purple

Zǐ

紫

Gray

灰 Huī

Gold

Jīn 金

Turquoise

Lán lǜ

蓝绿

Brown

棕 Zōng

Black 黑 Hēi

Maroon

栗Lisè

Teapot

This Chinese teapot is made of clay and used to brew tea. A popular tea for the Chinese New Year is oolong.

Chrysanthemum

During the Chinese New Year, the chrysanthemum flower is brought home for its vibrant colors, which represent happiness and prosperity.

Lucky Gold Coin

Lucky gold coins are used to commemorate the Chinese New Year. Some have the image of a zodiac animal for the corresponding year of issue.

Lucky Fish Symbol

Fish combine with Chinese characters to represent good fortune and happiness. Chinese people eat carp during the New Year to invite good fortune.

Firecrackers

Firecrackers are heard throughout the Chinese New Year. The sound is believed to scare away evil spirits.

Lucky Bamboo

The bamboo plant is believed to help ensure a harmonious long life. It is given as a gift during the Chinese New Year.

Paper Fan

Paper fans are a popular Chinese New Year wall decoration.

Tangerine

In Chinese culture, the tangerine represents wealth and happiness. During the Chinese New Year, tangerines are used as housewarming gifts.

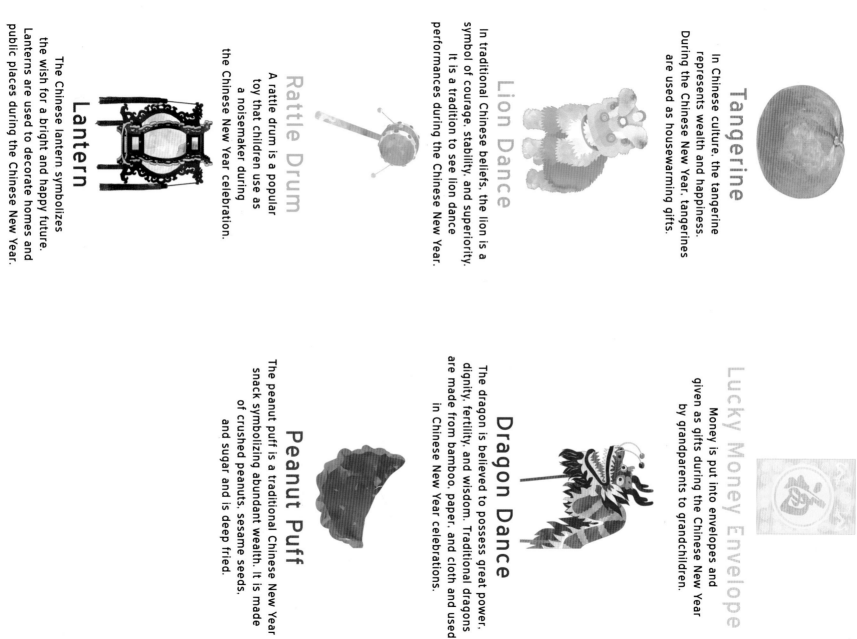

Lion Dance

In traditional Chinese beliefs, the lion is a symbol of courage, stability, and superiority. It is a tradition to see lion dance performances during the Chinese New Year.

Rattle Drum

A rattle drum is a popular toy that children use as a noisemaker during the Chinese New Year celebration.

Lantern

The Chinese lantern symbolizes the wish for a bright and happy future. Lanterns are used to decorate homes and public places during the Chinese New Year.

Lucky Money Envelope

Money is put into envelopes and given as gifts during the Chinese New Year by grandparents to grandchildren.

Dragon Dance

The dragon is believed to possess great power, dignity, fertility, and wisdom. Traditional dragons are made from bamboo, paper, and cloth and used in Chinese New Year celebrations.

Peanut Puff

The peanut puff is a traditional Chinese New Year snack symbolizing abundant wealth. It is made of crushed peanuts, sesame seeds, and sugar and is deep fried.